Passive Income

Best Business Ideas on How to Make Money and Create Financial Freedom

Jeffrey Turpen

Summary

The exciting world of passive income is the focus of this valuable book. Read on to learn about how passive income works.

This is a form of income that entails very little effort on your part over time. It requires a bit of an investment and some actual effort at the start but after a while it becomes all the more beneficial. This effort at the start typically involves creating a base for earning money.

The money you earn comes from sales of products or services you offer, advertising revenues, referral points and much more. The ways how you can earn money through passive income are indeed varied.

This guide will give you information on how to make money through passive income. Exercises are included in each chapter to help you see what you can do to get money and make any kind of passive income plan work to your benefit.

Your Gift!

We want to show our appreciation that you support our work, so we have put together a gift for you.

Just visit the link on the last page of this book to download it now.

We know you will love this gift.

Thanks!

Table of Content

INTRODUCTION	5
CHAPTER 1 – SELL AN EBOOK	7
Points For Making a Book	8
Marketing Your Book	9
Exercise	9
CHAPTER 2 – CREATE A BLOG	11
How Do You Earn Money?	12
Tips For Your Blog	12
Exercise	13
CHAPTER 3 – CREATE A REVIEW SITE	15
Points For Creating a Review Site	15
Avoiding Bias	17
Exercise	18
CHAPTER 4 – CREATE AN APP	19
Points For Creating An App	19
Derivative Apps Are Useful	20
Can An Outside Party Help?	21
Exercise	22

CHAPTER 5 – PRODUCT DESIGN — 23
What Products Can You Sell? — 24
Tips For Designs — 24
Exercise — 25

CHAPTER 6 – CREATE YOUTUBE VIDEOS — 26
What Are Your Videos About? — 28
How Many Videos? — 29
Can You Choose Your Sponsor? — 29
Exercise — 30

CHAPTER 7 – RENTING OUT ITEMS — 31
A Word of Caution — 33
Exercise — 34

CONCLUSION — 36

Introduction

You can make money online in a variety of ways but some of the best options involve ones that you don't have to put in much of an effort for. The exciting world of passive income is something you need to explore as it provides you with a great way to make money without doing much in the process.

Passive income is one of the more intriguing points of making money that you could ever consider. This refers to income that you earn from some investment or other work endeavor in which you are not actively involved in.

Here's an example of how passive income works in general. Let's say that you have some property, website or another item that you own or operate. You might have other people use it or access it in some other way.

But the key is that you would not have anything to do with the regular operations or management of the assets that you hold. Rather, you are letting out your investment to others.

Over time you will eventually make money off of that investment or other opportunity. The best part is that you will not have done all that much to keep it running. That is, you are earning money in the background.

Of course, this is just one of the ways how you could earn passive income. Several options are listed in this guide.

The potential for you to earn money through passive income is significant. There are no limits as to what you can earn. But to get the most money, you have to know what to do and how to do it the right way.

This guide will help you recognize the many ways how you can earn passive income. These include many solutions that are simple and easy to follow.

Each chapter ends with an exercise to help you figure out how you can complete a specific task. This is to help you fully understand how to get a quality passive income project to work.

The options for passive income are vast and worthwhile. Let's take a look at what you can do.

Chapter 1 – Sell an Ebook

People are always interested in reading. If anything, today's digital devices have only made it easier for people to read, what with them being able to load up electronic books. Selling a book is always a smart idea to consider.

It is very easy to sell ebooks online. Places like Amazon have become especially popular for how they allow people to list their own books online and sell them.

With such a setup, you will make money by getting a cut of the sales from each book you have. The place that hosts your book sale will end up getting a part of the sales as it is responsible for putting your book out there.

There is a good potential for you to make a great deal of money after you write a book and post it online. Best of all, you don't necessarily have to make something far too long. A book that is only around 50 to 80 pages – or even something as long as this book – will be good enough. The key is to write something that is appealing to people in some way.

Points For Making a Book

As you write a book, you have to think about how you will make it stand out and visible. To start, think about the subject that your book will cover. Look at what you might be interested in writing about and what you feel is appealing to audiences. Don't just write about anything; write about something that you know is worthwhile and is of interest to you. Be invested in your work.

Also, you should look at the kind of book you will write. While it is true that fictional works can be entertaining, books about certain real life topics or tutorials on how to do special things are appealing.

For instance, if you enjoy gardening then maybe you could use your knowledge of that field and put it into a book. It would be even better if you have a very specific field of work or interest to write about. This could include points relating to how to grow certain types of vegetables or how to maintain a garden during the winter season.

You also have to ensure the book is detailed and long enough. Don't try and make your ebook as long as a massive paperback novel. You don't need to make something that long just to earn passive income.

Marketing Your Book

After you are done writing your book, market it on social media, blog sites and other spots of value. The key is to market your work at places where people who might be interested in your book would see your messages at.

Going back to the gardening example, you would be better off marketing that book on blogs dedicated to the subject.

Be willing to answer questions that people might pose to you when you are promoting your book. Show them that you can answer questions that come about at any time.

Exercise

To prepare your book, think about what you are interested in writing on. After that, see if you can narrow down that interest to a very specific niche.

Look at the points you might want to highlight in your book. Prepare a good outline for that book as you start to write it. Make sure it is concise and sensible without going overboard.

Check on how well the book looks after you are finished writing it. Don't publish something that might appear unprofessional or poorly edited.

After writing your book, make sure it is loaded up onto the proper websites that sell ebooks. Amazon is obviously a good choice but look around elsewhere too. Be sure to also promote your work on blogs, social media sites and so forth to drum up interest.

Create multiple books if possible. Make them about the same niche or interest. Show that you've got a vested desire for something and that you want to share it with anyone who is interested.

Chapter 2 – Create a Blog

Are you interested in talking about all sorts of stuff? Maybe creating a blog is a great idea.

Blogging is appealing for how it provides people with a way to tell others about all sorts of things that they are interested in. A blog is great in that you can write about anything and update it as often as you want.

Do you want to create a blog relating to your favorite sports team? Maybe there's a music or movie genre you are interested in and you want to write about the newest developments in that field or about its history. There are no limits as to what you could talk about.

As you develop your blog, you will express yourself as an authority figure on something of value. Sharing your knowledge consistently and thoughtfully is important to do. This helps you show that you definitely understand whatever it is you want to highlight in your work.

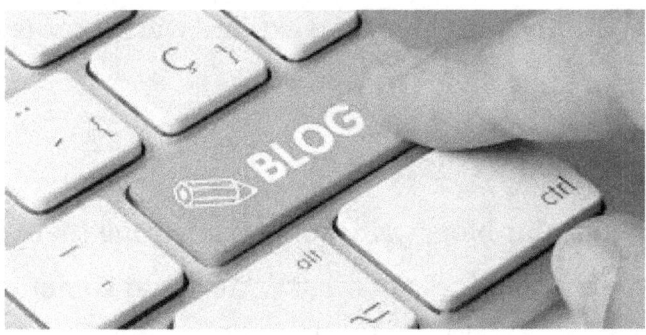

How Do You Earn Money?

You will earn more off of your blog through affiliate marketing. This is a process where you post a series of advertisements onto your site. These ads link to places that sell various items.

When a visitor clicks on an ad or link from your site, that person goes to a page through your referral link. That person orders a product or service within a certain timeframe. You then receive a substantial cut of the sale because you were the one that recommended a person to that site.

This is great provided that you have affiliate links that are relevant to whatever your blog is about. When you write about something relating to those links, it becomes easier for you to encourage people to visit those sites you are trying to steer them towards.

This comes as you are showing yourself as an authority on whatever you are blogging about. Write regularly about something you know and show your interest. Express to people that what you want to say is worthwhile and that there are plenty of intriguing things to explore with regards to something of importance to you.

Tips For Your Blog

When writing your blog, write about something that you are definitely interested in. Don't just write about something popular that you might not be all that invested in.

Keep your blog updated regularly. Establish a sensible schedule where a certain number of updates will be produced in a given time. You could update your blog on specific days of the week or every two or three days, for instance. Keep that schedule consistent so people will know when to expect new stuff off of your site.

Allow people to share things on your blog. Offer plenty of social media connections on your site.

Create links between your site and other places that cover similar interests. The odds are there are plenty of people out there who are running their own websites who want to share their likes and values.

Most importantly, avoid making your site look like a deliberate attempt at making money. Any links that you put into your site should be incorporate naturally without sounding like you're writing blatant advertisements.

Exercise

To establish a blog, find a proper hosting site. There are various free sites that will help you to host a blog.

You also have the option to create your blog through a website creator. Various programs such as this offer plug-ins and interface setups to help you create a visually stunning site. The cost associated with using such a creator will vary though. Watch for the costs involved with getting a domain name for the blog set up too.

Figure out a few posts that you want to produce. After that, create a schedule for when you are going to get those posts out. Make sure the schedule is consistent and regular.

Chapter 3 – Create a Review Site

Shopping has changed in the past few years. Today people go online to find information on things they want to order. Customers want to get details on as many items as possible. It is all about finding products that they know are worthwhile and are easy to enjoy.

There are many websites out there that let you compare different types of products or services. You might see a site that compares numerous computer antivirus programs. You could also see a place that reviews airline reward and loyalty plans.

Creating your review or comparison site is great for passive income. Such a site gives you the opportunity to use various affiliate programs to earn money. You will also provide visitors with a sensible service where people can understand everything in a certain category.

When you establish a review site, you will post links to sites where people can buy those products or services from. Make sure you sign up for their affiliate programs so you are properly rewarded though.

Points For Creating a Review Site

As you establish your review site, you will have to watch for how well the page is organized. You will have to post several products of a certain type on your site.

Your page will only work if you actually understand whatever it is you are trying to discuss. Reliable review sites are always written by people with a vested interest in in the things they want to talk about. Share information on what you know and give readers the opportunity to purchase items.

Consider the type of product or service you plan on reviewing. Choose an option that you know you are invested in or is something you understand.

Check up on different products that are available in that category. You don't necessarily have to buy them; you just need to look and see what these feature and how they might be different from one another. Create a series of categories that you will review and compare items based on.

Aim to get as many products as possible. Always use the newest products that are available in your reviews.

Update the site as often as needed when new things come out on the market. Letting people know about the latest items in a certain field is important as it gives you the opportunity to inform people about something of value.

Don't forget to add updates on any existing things that you have already discussed on your site.

Don't forget to include plenty of visual bits of information around your site. Pictures or screenshots of something are useful provided that you can get the copyrights or clearances to use them. Charts and other helpful visual aids especially make it easier for people to compare items and see what makes them different from each other.

Avoiding Bias

Biases are concerning problems that might come about when you're trying to create a review site. People might assume that you are biased towards one particular product or service. The concern is especially clear if you like one particular option that you are reviewing over all others.

You must ensure that you look at all items you review on your own. Avoid taking in money or other free offers from outside parties. The offers would often try and influence your opinion and might provide you with information that is heavily skewed in its favor.

Read the language you use on your website as well. Using extreme adjectives or overly positive or negative language can be a dangerous concern.

Be certain when writing that you check on everything you prepare. Think about whether some of the things you are writing are outlandish or if they are sensible.

Also, cover both the pros and cons of whatever you are writing about. Do not skew heavily towards one or two concepts or else it might be difficult for you to write something.

Exercise

To create a review or comparison site, start by looking at a certain topic or niche you have a strong interest in. Maybe you know of some field that you have used several products or services in.

Create a series of categories and other factors that you will compare and review individual products by. Use a series of subjects that are relevant to the matter.

Prepare an affiliate program with a particular place that sells certain items. Amazon has the most commonly used affiliate program that you can work with for your review site although you are free to look around to see what else is available for your use.

Chapter 4 – Create an App

Have you taken a look at the Google Play Store or the Apple App Store lately? You might notice that there are loads of different apps out there.

These include apps for everything. You can find some that focus on budgeting your money or organizing lists. You could also find some gaming apps that focus on a vast variety of activities.

Did you know that you can create an app to get passive income? This is possible as you will get a significant amount of money for every time that someone purchases and downloads your app.

Points For Creating An App

To earn passive income when creating an app, you have to think about a good program that you wish to create. You have to option to create any kind of app that you want but you should still think about how well such a program is to be run. The functionality of the program is critical to its success. Create a program that you know has a potential audience. Make the app run to where it will not be too hard to use.

As you create your app, look at how that program will be organized. Create an outline for that program based on what you want to incorporate into the setup.

The app must be distinct and appealing. More importantly, the program should also stand out in some manner. With so many apps out there, it is easy for yours to be lost in the pile of other programs for download. Create apps that you know will be visible and stand out in a special manner.

Derivative Apps Are Useful

One option to look into when creating an app is to think about a derivative app. This is a type of program which is similar to another app but has been redesigned or targeted to fit the needs of another party.

For instance, an app that helps with designing landscapes for the outside of a home could be reprogrammed to focus on how to design a den or basement or other large room inside a home. Anything could work if you think carefully about how you are targeting a specific group.

Can An Outside Party Help?

There are times when you might need some extra help for getting a mobile app ready. Maybe your ideas are a little more complex or you have very little technical knowledge for how to set up a program. But the cost of such services might be too high depending on how intense the support you need might be.

You could always contact freelance help or an app creator business to help you with setting up a quality app. Such services will analyze your needs and prepare a technically functional program that is right for you.

Many app production teams manage coding functions to create apps that run properly. More importantly, they are apps that work on a variety of mobile devices.

Outside parties can also assist you in getting such apps loaded onto proper marketplaces. A full listing that includes keywords, descriptions and screenshots of your app will be created by someone and submitted to the Google Play and Apple App Stores.

Such an outside service works if you have a great idea and you know everything you want to incorporate in your work. But to make this run right, you must look at the cost associated with the service. Compare the cost versus the potential profits you would get off of the app.

Depending on the estimated cost, it might be best for you to just learn how to create a good app through a certain program.

Exercise

To start, find a program that allows you to create an app. There are various software programs to choose from including Appery.io, Mobile Roadie, TheAppBuilder, Appy Pie and AppMachine. All of these programs give you a variety of options for preparing your own apps although the cost for getting one of these to work will vary.

After that, read on about how the program works. As you do this, consider the type of app you will prepare. Look at the goals you want to get out of it and how you would envision people making that app.

Establish an outline for the app and then prepare it based on what you feel is appropriate for its use. Check on how well the program is to be run so you will have a clear idea of how it might work.

Chapter 5 – Product Design

Today you could design a variety of products if you have the skills. You might be an artist who has many designs for shirts, for instance. You could also design websites with particular templates or schemes that can be appropriated by other people.

Product design jobs are appealing passive income options. This is a great process that works with a few important steps.

To start, come up with a design template for something of value. Think about how a template for a website could be utilized, for instance. Look at how the site might be arranged or how individual bars, columns and other features are organized.

After you come up with a design you must go and sell that to someone who will offer products or services that incorporate the design. For the website design template, send it off to a site that sells such options for those who wish to create their own pages.

As the product is available, you will get a profit off of sales relating to that design. Every time someone buys what you have, you will earn a cut of the profits. This adds up over time and gives you a huge payout after a while.

What Products Can You Sell?

The things that you could sell are especially worthwhile. Design templates can be easily prepared and offered to websites that cater to people aiming to create their own pages. Meanwhile, art designs for shirts, laptop covers, cell phone cases and stickers could be sent to many crafts sites. These places take your design patterns and print them onto a variety of items. The designs are typically printed on demand as sometimes such designs might not be big enough to where they could be mass-produced.

Over time, you will get loads of money when you have plenty of designs available. Creating unique and distinctive designs does more than show off your intriguing style. It also gives people different options for showing off their interests. The fashionable designs of what you have to offer will make a real difference.

Tips For Designs

Look at your creativity skills. Are you are great cartoon artist? Maybe you are good with promotional art. Whatever the case, focus your designs based on things you have a strong vested interest in.

After this, look for a niche of value to you. It might be interesting to create artistic designs that focus on a variety of specifics that are interesting. You might be impressed at how different topics can be represented by unique designs.

Exercise

Think about an artistic design that might be appealing. Choose a design plan that reflects what you like and what you enjoy doing. Be creative when coming across something that stands out and offers a distinct look into your psyche.

Create a few drafts of a design before submitting it to a website. Look at the design and think about how it would look. Does this look like it would be great on a coffee mug? Would it fit on a shirt? Could it display well on a web browser?

After refining your design a few times, send it out to a website that takes in such items. Choose a proper firm based on what you wish to make out of your artistic creation.

Chapter 6 – Create YouTube Videos

YouTube is one of the most exciting websites around. It has become the top place for online videos for how it offers a variety of things for people to watch. From self-help and instructional videos to historic or informative files, people can enjoy YouTube for a variety of fun things. There are many entertaining videos that cover movies, video games and much more as well.

But some of the more popular YouTube videos are from people who have made names for themselves on the site. It seems as though people these days are becoming famous on YouTube. They just post a bunch of videos of themselves doing stuff and the next thing you know they are all over the place.

It is obvious that you aren't necessarily going to make millions of dollars off of YouTube videos like what so many others do. But you can still create YouTube videos with the intention of making money.

This comes from the advertising revenue that you will get off of those videos. Original videos can include advertisements that appear at varying times. They might appear before a video starts playing or in the middle. In other cases ads come in the form of popups that appear at random.

A YouTube user who has ads on one's videos will earn money for each time those messages are viewed. This total adds up over time to an extensive amount.

You don't have to become a massive YouTube celebrity to make passive income off of the site. But it does help to look at a few points for getting YouTube to work to your advantage.

What Are Your Videos About?

Create videos that are entertaining or informative. Make ones that are worthwhile based on what you are interested in. It is clear that you must work on content that you actually have a vested interest in. You don't want to make videos if you have no idea what you are discussing or you have no interest in the subject matter.

But when think about your interests, you should see if they are ones that are worth sharing with others. You might have an interest in playing a certain small-level sport like ultimate Frisbee or curling, for instance. Creating videos about those is great for how you are not only highlighting what you like but are also bringing it out to people who might be interested in such activities. These include people who are familiar with them and those who want to learn a little something more about your interests.

Search for your interests on YouTube to see if other people are covering them already. Look at what their videos are about in particular. As you do this, come up with unique ideas that have not been covered by those videos. You could fill in the gaps that have been left by all those people on YouTube.

How Many Videos?

Be advised when trying to create YouTube videos that you will need plenty of them for your efforts to be successful. You must get dozens of them ready for your site to become a trustworthy and appealing place for people to visit.

Keep on posting videos on a regular basis just to become visible. Having one or two in a week is always a good idea.

It can take a while to get all those videos that you want added onto your site. But when done right, it becomes easier for you to make money off of your YouTube channel.

Can You Choose Your Sponsor?

One issue to consider about using YouTube for passive income is that you might not always have the option to stick with certain kinds of sponsors. It most cases you have to only work with one or two particular sponsors. These are based on who is spending the most money to get onto YouTube.

Over time, your YouTube channel will become a little more recognized. The keywords on your videos and the links that come into and out of those videos will pair up with particular advertisements. Such ads are more relevant to your needs and the desires of the people who want the videos.

When those ads become relevant, people are more likely to click on their links. They may also be more likely to actually watch those ads and not click the skip button to get straight to your video. Your potential for profits will increase when people actually interact with or watch those ads. But again, this only works when people watch your videos on a regular basis.

Exercise

Look at what you are interested in and create plans for videos based on that interest. Plan out some topics you want to discuss. Create individual videos for each of those topics or subjects to introduce.

Record videos that are carefully orchestrated. Establish a script for each video and check on the technical features of each video. Everything you prepare should be professional in its appearance. Don't upload stuff that looks like you just spent a few minutes throwing everything together.

As you create those videos, plan a schedule for when each of those videos will be introduced. Look at how you will post them based on their descriptions too.

When this works, your YouTube page becomes more interesting. It especially comes as people notice that you are a more reliable and trustworthy source for information on something.

Chapter 7 – Renting Out Items

The last of the options to look into for earning passive income involves taking assets that you already have and letting people use them. The process requires a bit of effort on your hand as it requires you to have particular assets on hand. But it could provide you with passive income as it works.

With this, you will allow other people to enjoy what you have and make money off of it. You don't even have to be around for people to take in your items.

You have probably been hearing about crowd sharing in recent time. With people looking for ways to save money on accommodations, vehicle rentals and such, they are turning to everyday people for help.

They know that rentals are cheaper when they contact people directly through crowd sharing websites. The variety of things available for rent is also greater. A car rental company can only offer so many types of vehicles.

With crowd sharing, a person could go online and find any car that could be rented out. The vehicle could be a basic passenger car for a long business trip. Maybe the car might be something fancy that could be rented out for a wedding. Whatever the case is, the selection that someone has should be greater when going online.

For instance, you could rent out your home to someone while you are out of town or you could allow someone to stay in a room for a period of time. You might also make a vehicle in your garage accessible to someone for a few hours at a time. Anything that is lying around in your home or is not used could provide you with passive income in the form of people renting out what you have.

A plan for renting out items works with a few steps. First, you will go to a site that allows you to list items that you want to rent out. Places like Airbnb have become very popular for this purpose.

You would have to list details on whatever it is you want to rent out to people. It might include something like a spare room in your home that is not used all that often. Maybe you have a vehicle that is not used regularly and could be offered to someone else for a bit.

As you rent these items out, you would charge people a certain amount of money for using them. That total would vary based on the particular items you are renting out and the money you agree to charge.

You will earn a particular total based on the charge that the site incorporates plus the fees that the hosting site that you list your item on charges. The totals can add up over time if you regularly let out something to other people.

A Word of Caution

As appealing as this option might be, you would have to watch for the terms associated with letting out items to other people. Make sure you only offer items that you know are safe to let other people use.

Watch for how you are maintaining whatever you have to provide to clients. You must keep your home, car or other property that you will make available in the best possible condition.

This is to not only ensure it is suitable for use but also to show clients that you care. It is often easier to make money this way if you show that you put in enough effort for letting products out in a responsible manner.

Also, look at how often you would plan on offering your items. You don't want to chase people off by needing to share things at a certain time that might be inconvenient for some.

Many places that let you rent things out give you the option to keep certain items off limits for specific periods of time. These include cases where you need to use something for yourself and you cannot get anyone else to use an item for a particular time.

Also, any contracts involved with the rental process should be understood and analyzed. Review what a website or other rental service provider will demand from you.

Exercise

Look at a space in your home or other large item that could be made available for someone. Do you use a certain room all that often? Is there a vehicle that just lies there in your garage? Perhaps you have some yard equipment that could be made available.

Figure out what is dormant in your space and find a site that lets you list items available for rent in your local area. Look at the available times you have for letting people use something. Keep whatever is listed properly maintained. Check all parts of whatever you are offering and clean off anything that you've got.

Take pictures to show that what you have is functional and appealing. Those pictures should go right on your online listing.

Think about some questions that people might ask about whatever you are offering. Look for answers relating to how certain items are to be offered and be prepared to address them.

As you come across the right plans, you will find that it is not too hard to get passive income over the things that you already have in your home. Take advantage of whatever is just sitting around and find ways to make them more visible and useful. The money you will get off of them will add up after a while.

Conclusion

All of these ideas for getting the most out of your passive income plans are worth exploring. The chances that you have for getting money without putting in much effort over time will be worthwhile.

You must look into how well your plans for making passive income work though. Be certain you take a look at what you will be setting up in your process. Be aware of how you might have to spend some money to get a few of these plans running depending on what you might be working with.

Maintaining your passive income efforts is also important to consider. You must look at how well the income streams you take in are operated so they will be easy to follow.

Don't forget to think about how you will tackle some of these endeavors. Being creative and thoughtful in your plans will go a long way. It only takes a few bits of time at the start to give you a lifelong stream of income that can add up.

Good luck with your efforts in getting the most out of your passive income plans.

Your Gift!

We want to show our appreciation that you support our work, so we have put together a gift for you.

bit.ly/2u7pdNL

Just visit the link above to download it now.

We know you will love this gift.
Thanks!

www.ingramcontent.com/pod-product-compliance
Lightning Source LLC
Chambersburg PA
CBHW050252230526
45470CB00005B/2237